HILARIOUS JOKES

FOR

YEAR OLD KIDS

What do you call a fake noodle?

An IMPASTA

Why did the banana go to the doctor's office?

He wasn't peeling very well!

What animals have to wear wigs?

BALD Eagles

What makes ghosts bad liars?

You can see right through 'em!

What's a cow with no legs called?

Ground beef

What do you call cheese that doesn't belong to you?

Na-cho cheese

Where do cows like to go to on the weekends?

The moooooovies

What is an alligator in a vest called?

An investigator

What is a man with a shovel called?

Doug

Why didn't the pinata want any dessert?

Because he was already stuffed!

What kind of eggs do evil hens like to lay?

Deviled eggs

What did one plate say to the other?

Dinner's on me!

Why did the cookie go to the doctor?

Because she was feeling crumby.

What did the traffic light say to the waiting car?

Don't look, I'm changing!

What elementary subject do witches like the most?

Spelling

Why can't you give Elsa a balloon to hold onto?

Because she will <u>let it go</u>!

Why do bees tend to have sticky hair?

Because they use honey combs!

What's the cross between a vampire and snowman?

Frostbite

Why is the math workbook always so sad?

Because it has lots of problems.

What's a sleeping bull called?

A bull<u>dozer</u>

Why do sharks have to swim in saltwater?

Pepper water is irritating!

Where do fish like to store their money?

In the river bank

What does a cloud wear under it's pants?

Thunderwear

What did one snowman say to the other?

You smell carrots?

What kind of music do balloons hate?

Pop music

What kind of room doesn't have doors?

A mushroom

Why was the golfer wearing 2 pants?

In case he got a hole in one!

What's the best way to make a tissue dance?

By putting a little boogey in it!

What did the girl toilet say to the boy toilet?

You look flushed!

What stays in a corner yet travels around the world?

A stamp

What did the dad spider complain to his son about?

Too much time on the web!

Why was the baby strawberry sad?

His dad was in a jam!

What do you call your dad when he's frozen?

Popsicle

What do you call someone that has no body or nose?

Nobody knows!

What do vegetarian
zombies like to eat?
GRRRRRRAAAAAAIIIIIINNSSSS

What's the Easter Bunny's
favorite breakfast spot?
IHOP

What do you call a rabbit that tells good jokes?

A funny bunny

What do call a dog that can do magic?

A Labracadabrador

What did the ice cream say to the chocolate?

You're sweet!

Why couldn't the motorcycle stand up?

It was two tired!

What did the dad buffalo after dropping his son off?

Bi-son

Where do college aged vampires like to shop?

Forever 21

What's the loudest pet available?

A trumpet

Why was the bunny in a terrible mood?

He had a bad hare day.

Why haven't you learned the alphabet?

I don't know why (y)!

Where does Christmas come before Easter?

In the dictionary

Why did the boy throw his clock out the window?

He wanted to see time fly!

How does a train like to eat?

By going chewwww chewww!

What's another name for a bear without teeth?

A gummy bear

What's a snake's favorite subject?

Hissssstory

What's a cow's favorite holiday?

Moooo Year's Eve

Why are cats not good storytellers?

Because they only have 1 tail!

Why did the shrimp refuse to share her treasure?

She was being a little shellfish!

How did the judge react to seeing the skunk?

By saying "Odor in the court!"

What did the asparagus say to the mushroom?

You're a fun-gi!

What kind of nut does not have a shell?

A doughnut

Why did the egg have such a serious face?

He was trying not to crack up!

What did the nut say when it caught a cold?

Caaaashewwww

What kind of chocolate do astronauts like the most?

Mars

What did the volcano say to his wife?

I lava you!

Why is 6 so afraid of 7 all the time?

Because 7-8-9.

What is a robot's favorite snack?

Computer chips

What kind of witches like the beach?

Sand-witches

What's a pirate's favorite restaurant?

Arrrrby's

How do trees access the internet?

By logging in

How are billboards able to talk?

By using sign language

What has three letters and starts with gas?

A car

What gets wetter and wetter the more it dries?

A towel

What letter in the alphabet do pirates like?
ARRRRRRRR

Why couldn't the pirate learn the alphabet?
Because he got lost at C!

Why did the child bring a ladder to school?

To go to <u>high</u> school!

What type of shoes do ninjas love?

<u>Sneakers</u>

What is Thanos's favorite app?

Snapchat

Why should you be careful telling a joke around glass?

Because it might crack up!

How did Ben Franklin feel when he discovered electricity?

He was shocked!

Why should you never tell a joke about pizza?

Because it's too cheesy!

What kind of music do mummies love?

Wrap music

Why is it so windy inside of a stadium?

Because of all the fans!

Why do vampires always seem so sick?

Because they're always coffin!

What did the fisherman say to the magician?

Pick a cod, any cod!

Where were pencils invented?

Pencil-vania

Why should you never trust a zoo keeper?

Because they love cheetahs!

How come the duck couldn't pay for dinner?

Her <u>bill</u> was too big!

Where do you learn to make ice cream?

Sundae school

What kind of tree can fit in your hand?

A <u>palm</u> tree

Where do hamburgers like to go to dance?

The meat<u>ball</u>

How do elves learn spelling?

By memorizing the elfabet

What is a skeleton's favorite instrument?

A trom<u>bone</u>

What kind of weather do kings enjoy the most?

Reign

Why isn't Cinderella allowed to play soccer?

Because she always runs away from the ball!

Why couldn't the music teacher start his car?

His keys were on the piano!

How does Darth Vader like to have his toast?

On the dark side

What make spiders great at web development?

Their ability to find bugs!

Which sort of bugs do the CIA like the most?

Spy-ders

How was the barber able to win the race?

By taking the <u>short</u>cut!

What did the hat say to his friend?

I'm going on a<u>head</u>.

What's the best thing to put into a pie?

Your teeth

How come the broom was late to the party?

It over-swept.

How do pirates like to stay in touch with one another?

Via sea-mail

How did the scarecrow secure the promotion?

By being outstanding in his field

What cereal do rodents love to eat?

Mice krispies

Why did the Scot have plumbing problems?

Because he only had bagpipes!

Knock Knock
Who's there?
Noah
Noah who?
Noah good place to go grab a
bite to eat?

Knock Knock
Who's there?
Avenue
Avenue who?
Avenue heard me knock
before?

Knock Knock
Who's there?
Annie
Annie who?
Annie thing that you can do,
I can do better

Knock Knock
Who's there?
Abby
Abby who?
Abby birthday to you!

Knock Knock
Who's there?
Police
Police who?
Police let us inside, it's
freezing out here!

Knock Knock
Who's there?
Woo
Woo who?
What are you so excited
about?

What do you get when you put cheese next to ducks?

Cheese and quackers

What's a fatigued pea called?

Sleep-pea

Knock Knock
Who's there?
Kanga
Kanga who?
Kanga Roo

Knock Knock
Who's there?
Canoe
Canoe who?
Canoe do my homework for me?

What did the elevator yell to his friend?

I'm falling!

What goes up but doesn't come back down?

Age

What'd the shark say after eating the clownfish?

This tastes funny...

What's the best way to throw a space party?

Ya gotta planet!

Hey pssst did you hear that rumor about butter?
Never mind I shouldn't spread it.

Why don't scientists ever trust atoms?
They tend to make up everything!

Which kind of fish is the most expensive?

A goldfish

Why did a tulip grow from the cake?

Because it was made of flower!

Did you hear about the claustrophobic astronaut?

He really needed some space!

Why can't you ever trust stairs?

They're always up to something

What did the block say to his friend to leave?

Lego

What did the guitar say to the guitarist?

Quit stringing me along!

What's scarier than a monster?

A MOMster

Why did the garden feel so overcrowded?

There wasn't mushroom!

What's a student that despises math?

A calcu-hater

What do piglets use when they have a rash?

Oinkment

Thank you for reading! We hope everyone enjoyed the jokes and had lots of laughs!

As a special thank you for purchasing this book, please enjoy this exclusive preview from one of our other best sellers.

The Christmas Jokes Game Book

For Kids

How To Play

Step 1

Split into two teams whether that be boys vs girls, kids vs parents, or any mix of your choice. If possible, also assign one person as a referee. You can also do 1 vs 1!

Step 2

Decide who gets to go first. Which team can do the most pushups? Which team can guess the number between 1 and 10 from someone not playing the game? Or just a good old fashioned rock paper scissors?

Step 3

The starting team has to tell a joke from the book. You can say the joke however you like and animate it too with funny faces, gestures, voices or whatever else!

Step 4

If everyone on the opposing team laughs, the other team gets a point! Set a limit for how many points it takes to win and the first team to reach the limit, wins!

(Optional) Decide whether it will be a single game or best of 3, 5 or 7.

What language does Santa speak?

North Polish

What do reindeer say before telling their best jokes?

This will sleigh you!

Who is a Christmas tree's favorite singer?

Spruce Springsteen

What's red and white and keeps falling down chimneys?

Santa Klutz

Where do Christmas plants go to become movie stars?

Holly-wood

How does a cow like to say Merry Christmas?

Moowy Christmas

How did Scrooge win the football game?

The ghost of Christmas passed!

What do snowmen call their kids?

Chill-dren

What did the peanut butter say to the grape during the holidays?

Tis' the season to be jelly!

Why did the apple pie start crying?

Because its peelings were hurt.

How do Christmas angels greet each other?

By saying, "Halo!"

What did the ghost say to Santa?
I'll have a boo Christmas without you!

A Message From the Publisher

Hello! My name is Hayden and I am the owner of Hayden Fox Publishing, the publishing house that brought you this title.

My hope is that you enjoyed this book and had some fun and laughs on every page. If you did, please think about leaving a review for us on Amazon or wherever you purchased this book. It may only take a moment, but it really does mean the world for small businesses like mine.

Our mission is to create premium content for children that will help them build confidence, grow their imaginations, get away from screens, spend more quality time with family, and have lots of fun and laughs doing it. Without you, however, this would not be possible, so we sincerely thank you for your purchase and for supporting our company mission.

~ Hayden

Check out our other books!

For more, visit our Amazon store at:
amazon.com/author/haydenfox

Made in the USA
Monee, IL
14 December 2020